moonlight
monsters &morality
A REFLECTION OF LIFE, AS SEEN THROUGH THE JAUNDICED EYES OF A SINNER
By Simon Paul Ridgeway

Dedication

Acknowledgements

Firstly I would not have been able to complete this work, had it not been for the love and encouragement of an exceedingly courageous lady, my mother, Val.

It was she who spurred me on during those days of self-pity and introspection when I felt the volume of work would not come together. I was inspired by her belief in her children, that had no boundaries. Mom, could never say no, and when I sat with her to read the latest edited version, she would listen avidly and then ask pertinent questions. My mother was an inspiration to all she came into contact with, and her passing only recently had given me the impetus to finalise the book.

The work is a labour of love, and the hours I spent pouring over texts to ascertain historical correctness, was what inspired the poem 1642. I had been looking through the Concise Penguin dictionary for a spelling when I realized the enormity of that work, and truly appreciated how much labour had gone into its volumes. It was the number of pages in that book that I used for the title, a somewhat fitting tribute to the scale of size of Southern Africa and the complexity of its people and creatures.

With this in mind, the title of this work sprung from the pages when I had seen the index on its pages which had evoked the thought that our country was resplendent with all three aspects to our history. The title became the basis for the whole book, although it reinvigorated my work mostly in light of the second half.

To Lynda Gibson, who was harangued by my insistence that the poetry must somehow do justice to the history of the continent we have chosen as home, but needed to give hope to all who suffered under the yolk of tyranny displayed by uncaring monsters. This was not lost on any of us, and although it was the photography that brought it to life, the sheer immensity of the work that still has to be done is what drives us all.

The gentle folk of the Operation Relief Program who tirelessly feed the vast number of refugees who have chosen South Africa as their place of refuge, have inoculated me against the depressive conditions that these refugees live in, but have been a breath of fresh air, among a generally unflinching megalomania which constitutes itself in our populace. The sense of rage that inspired 'The greed of man' and 'To walk on lonely streets' gave me courage to speak my mind.

Thank you Tanya Carter for your belief and the hours you poured over the work and gave sense and purpose to why we were doing this. I am grateful for your undivided attention.

Lastly, to the people who inspired my voice of unrepentant empathy. Hopeful I am that in time you may return home to a country free from tyranny.

Foreword

What an honor for Simon to ask me to write the foreword for this wonderful compilation of Poetry that deals with issues so close to my heart.
I am always in awe of people who can write such moving poetry, seemingly effortlessly, about real and pertinent issues that we face in South Africa today.

I have known Simon almost forever and he never ceases to amaze me with his heart for the people of our country. He is always working on some worthy cause that makes a difference in the lives of so many oppressed and disadvantaged people. Simon has touched many with his unfailing love and patience. Never in the limelight, he has tirelessly worked away taking water and provisions to people in harsh, impoverished conditions or simply counselling a lost soul or walking a little old lady across the road in Parkhurst. Simon makes me smile; he brings light into dark situations never too busy or too tired to care.
Each generation has its' own seemingly insurmountable issues to deal with and Simon highlights some of ours, but never without hope. We are surrounded by pain, suffering and yet so much beauty. His poetry manages to see the joy and the pain, the magnificence of our land as well as the sadness.

Well done Simon, I salute you.

Marilyn Michau

Liberty

Bring to me the unwashed masses in a struggle to be free,
Lay them at my feet and I will give them liberty,
Provide for them that toil within the shadow of my hand,
To work in peace and strive to gain, the promise of that land.

Hold them in a grip of concrete plinth and stained iniquity,
Guide them on their way with strains of hope and dignity,
Raise to them a signal of your grand and masterful design,
And in return, they will reward the bounty of your time.

Grasp the weak and hungry in the spirit of your mark,
The time will show in grand design the shadow of your arc,
Gain for those your lofty core, in strength to hold them tight,
In whose palm you grip the rod, to clasp them with all might.

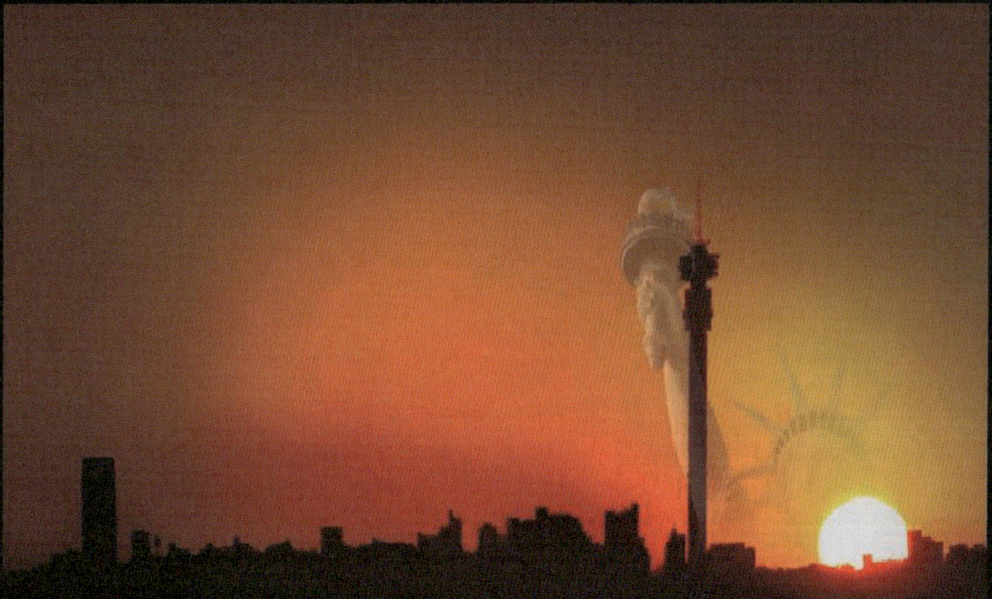

Call to them in long refrain the multitude you host,
Give to them that have no hope, the mirage of your post,
Stand alone and be assured, you beacon to the poor,
Harken back to days of old, the dream that you implore.

Hide them from the gallows, of a mis-spent time and place,
Where man has failed to understand the calling of his race,
Lift them from their motherland, to which they may alight,
And I will guide them on their way, when the time is right.

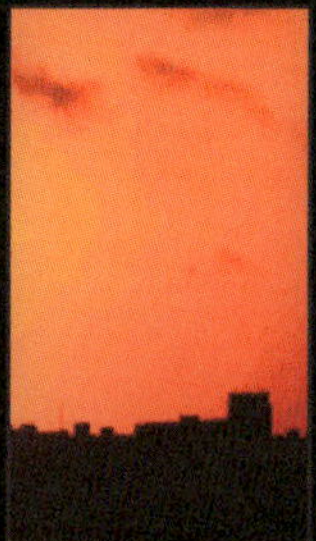

To Walk on Lonely Streets

To walk on lonely streets amidst the frail and faceless hungry,
To gaze upon those hopeless souls, each to all and sundry,
To drive upon those pot-holed roads amidst the endless plunder,
To look upon the blameless few and then to think and wonder.
To which of whom the blame resounds, but who is still aloof.
To what affect a few may have, when in the final proof,
To whom the shadow of misdeeds will fall, when time is nigh,
To stand along-side life-less men, the blame they would deny.

Johannesburg skyline

The Warzone

The Warzone

in a Josephanic veneer, the rolling cloud pronounces
Its boisterous African display
Their sycophantic play to the world
The drumbeat of thunder announces
A Kalashnikophonic refrain, of the hail of
On a Highveld sunlit day
The ricochet, of a war display
A valiant world would
The earsplitting resound, too illicit a sound
The symphonic chorus, replete
Enharmonic in beat, to the ear
Their rackety fall
On corrugated roof, to withstand them foolproof
The ice stones make their
Their lively ballet, in an unfolding
A Joburg afternoon
Then in concert retreat, the cattle
Their efforts fall on deaf
The folly a mere, moment
Only to

The Jacaranda

Amongst the jacaranda petals strewn on that dust laden path, a stairway to the rock of Peter, the hew of blue, a precursor of the sky.

The traveler amidst the noonday shadows, caste in contrast to the earthen heat of a pre-summer shower, lifts his head to the summit,

a submission to the grandeur of an African refrain.

The tree lined path stretches to the zenith of a kaleidoscope of shapes, man-made intrusions on the earth mother's belly.

d of grand illusions has stood the countless millennia of pre-history, in gentle anticipation. The onslaught of man's iniquities a testament to the tragedy that has

her gut for three hundred year and some.

The traveler on his lonely climb must first admit the injustice of this failed incursion, the foreigner on foreign soil, once provider, now viewed as that jacaranda,

A man to whom a lifetime of diligence and forlorn endeavour,
may never be admitted the key to that cast iron gate that stands an affront to a generation lost in the pursuit of kinship.
To stand alone, on that lofty hill, to gaze upon those unyielding vales,
to breathe the sweet air of an indistinct scent, wafting on a Southern African breeze.
The storm to come, a portent of the ground swell of common thought,
intent on erasing the contributions of generations,
distinct and unchallenged in its entirety; this storm must wash away the deep-rooted pedigree of this visitor,
or learn to live with its capacious canopy.
No longer an invader on a distant shore; the man may find solitude in the shade of its time worn sanctuary,
and solace in the value of its unfamiliar respite.

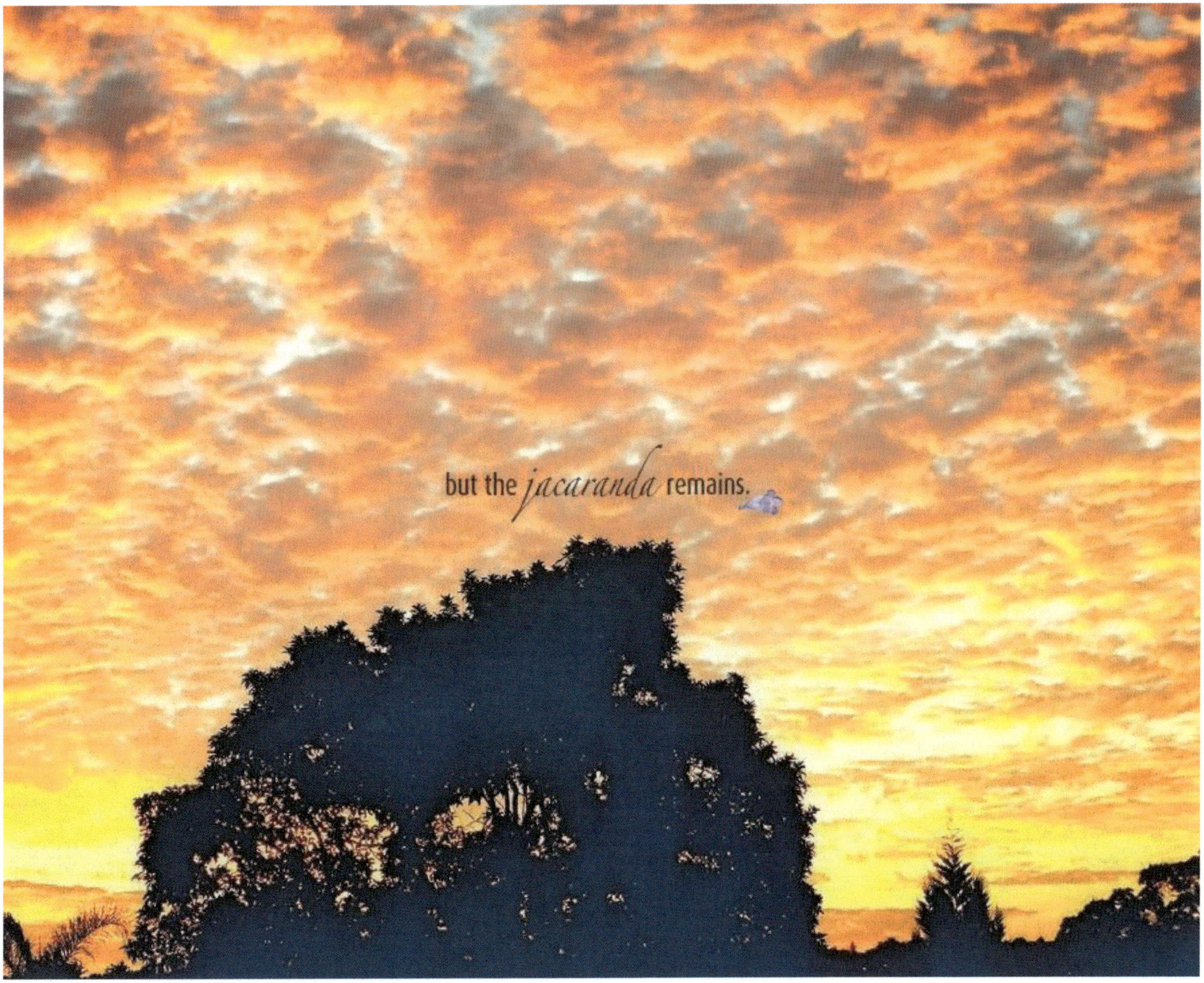
but the jacaranda remains.

Vaal River storms

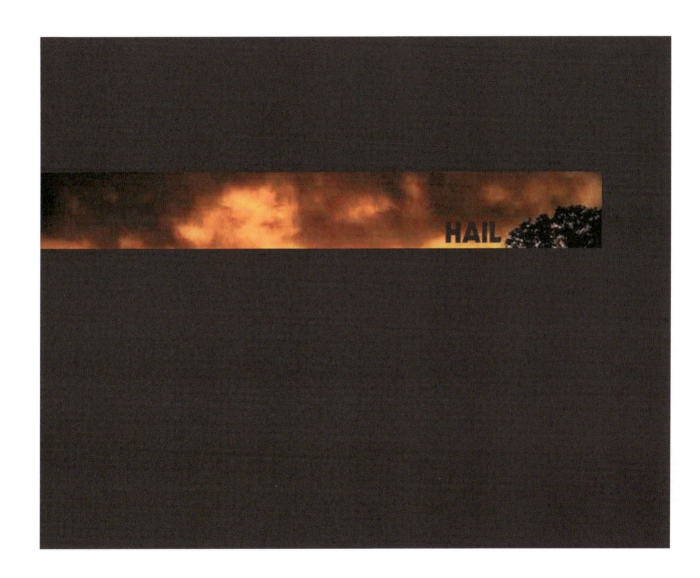
HAIL

The darkness appears on an eastern horizon, just as those ancient Impi may have emerged on distant plains, on long forg

e glory of a resurrected deluge, they appear in stark distinction to the fallow fields.

aves with growing immensity, a herald of the tide to come, an omen of that which will wreak havoc.

Along the buttressed hills, in anticipation of the coming onslaught, a gathering storm announces itself to an expectant world, proclaiming yet an

Draped as curtains on a foreboding stage, they hang suspended in Machiavellian anticipation.

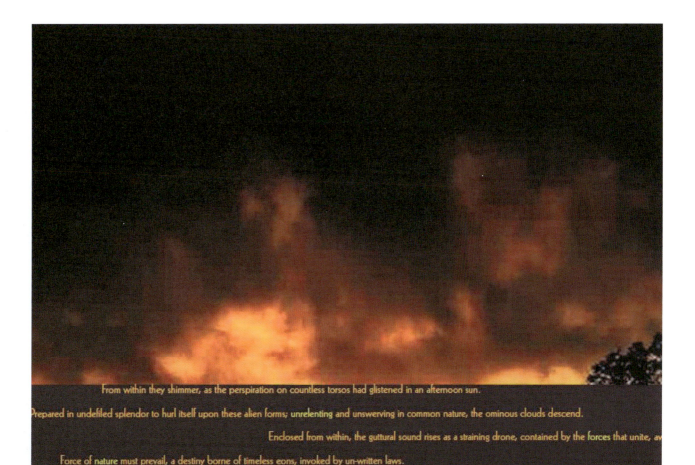

From within they shimmer, as the perspiration on countless torsos had glistened in an afternoon sun.

Prepared in undefiled splendor to hurl itself upon these alien forms; unrelenting and unswerving in common nature, the ominous clouds descend.

Enclosed from within, the guttural sound rises as a straining drone, contained by the forces that unite, av

Force of nature must prevail, a destiny borne of timeless eons, invoked by un-written laws.

Grandiose and unsurpassed they wait; fear suspended.

Then in calamitous union,

with one, the heavens open, the **blitz** begins.

First one, then the next in dreadful staggering, they are hurled in un-lamenting force, then crash as each must yield to the unmovable.

Smash and crack they wreak a trail of destruction on that which they visit; to fear, fear itself; a well-worn omen.

To dance rumba and prance in a dreadful liturgy, they must by all means pursue the element that evokes their natural heritage.

Un-deterred and **magnificent** they are cast onto the pasture of countless bounty, awaited and foreseen.

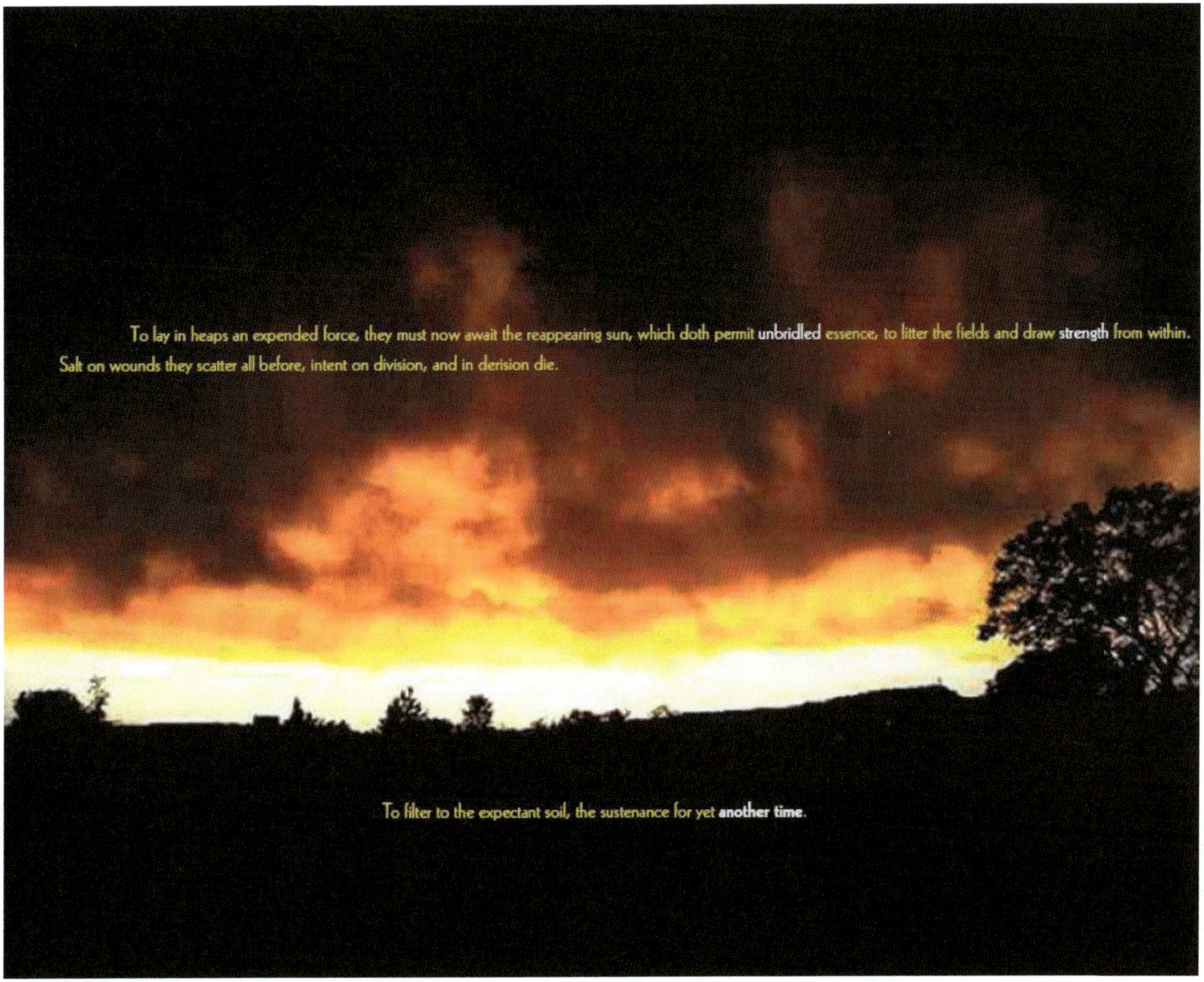
To lay in heaps an expended force, they must now await the reappearing sun, which doth permit unbridled essence, to litter the fields and draw strength from within.
Salt on wounds they scatter all before, intent on division, and in derision die.
To filter to the expectant soil, the sustenance for yet another time.

lightning

To visit on that mother load, to flash in seamless surge,
The workings of a natural act, upon that stage to purge,
The glory of an earthen heaven, with all its laden gold,
A story man with time forgot, its legend must be told.

The tortured flash in forks of grand and all forsaken light,
Ventured from the fearsome cloud a spear of celestial might,
To spew upon the rolling hills, and in the shady dale,
The awesome act in violent stabs, the earth it would impale.

The harsh contrast of flash, then gone, the crack a bold lament,
A shriek to all the world to see, the power that is spent,
To gaze upon the harsh bright flash, to watch its greatness grow,
And then again to marvel more, upon that splendid show.

Then dance across the bold black sky, a litany of lost dark souls,
The faces peer from every cloud, the eyes are pitch-black coal,
In every brief and ghastly blink, an intermittent call,
To those in whom the power lies, a post lapsarian fall.

The earth to which all power is drawn, a portent to the meek,
To not lose hope in all mankind, to those of whom we speak,
A prayer in jagged language spoke, an assault on the eye,
Emblazoned on the souls of men, across that jet-black sky.

Sunset over water

THE MINE

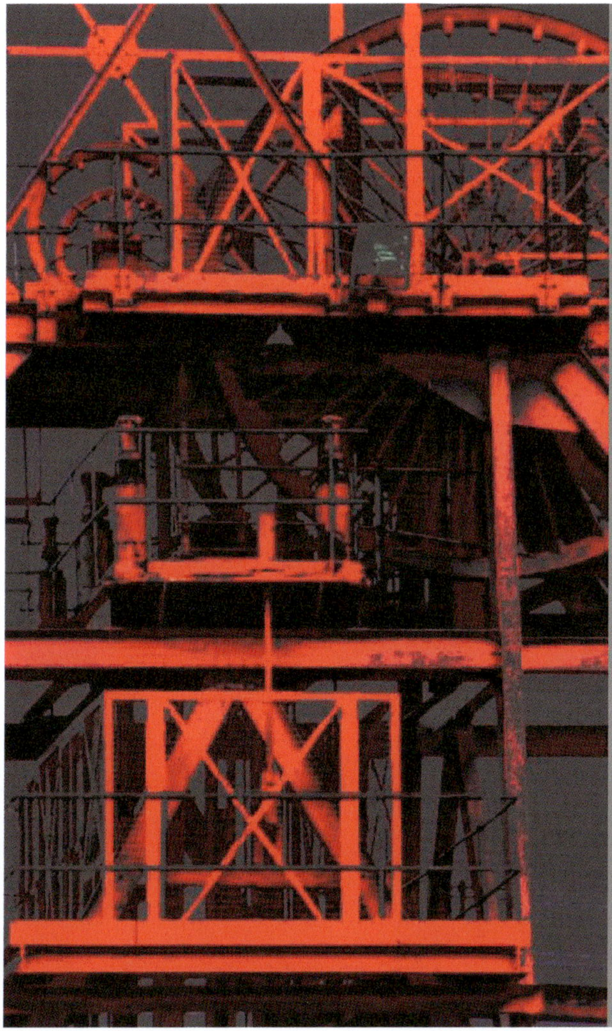

Warrens borne within the surrogate,
Where ageless creation would impregnate,
Deep within the landscape,
A vile reform, to proliferate.

Then break new ground they infiltrate,
The heaving mass to remonstrate,
With countless mode of corrugate,
Regard they must the concentrate.

To molten earth in aggregate,
Then rip the gut and stimulate,
The loathsome form, manipulate,
In gross defilement, they copulate.

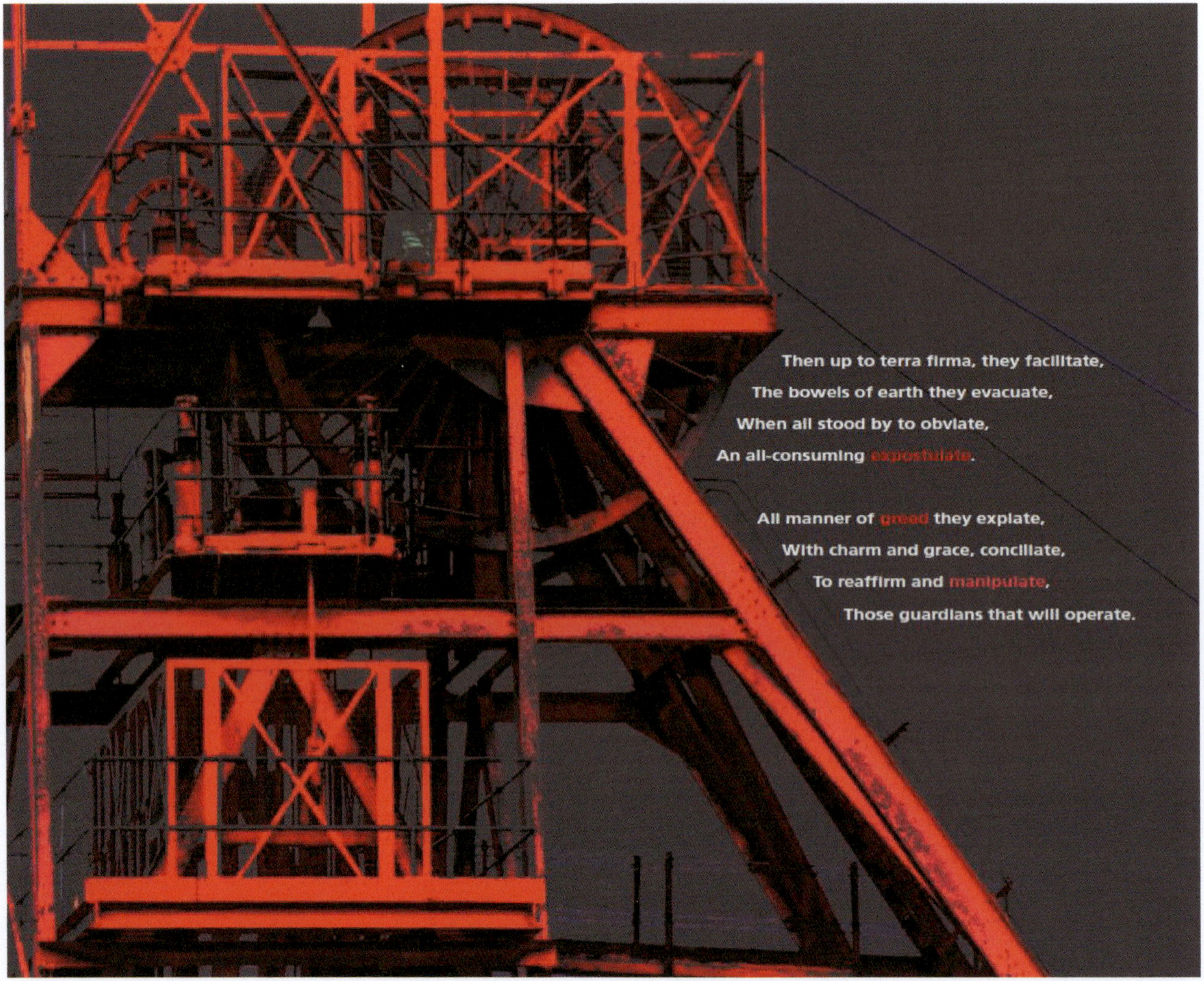

Then up to terra firma, they facilitate,
The bowels of earth they evacuate,
When all stood by to obviate,
An all-consuming expostulate.

All manner of greed they expiate,
With charm and grace, conciliate,
To reaffirm and manipulate,
Those guardians that will operate.

The Vulture

To soar above that vast and natural plain,

Where thermals guide the process of your reign,

To gaze upon the working, worrying kill,

Where shadows ride, in concert to your will.

To zoom your focus, fast on your domain,

Where telescopic sight directs you to contain,

To sense the willing, warming wanton thrill,

Where men might least to you, the re-instill.

To grasp the image, that you will have in vain,
Where all around you, sing your loud refrain,
To cast that shadow on the land you till,
Where once a time, in days gone by, stood still.

To that earthly soil, you glide, to once obtain,
Where men might guide you falsely in disdain,
To raise the bar that once they thought was ill,
Where, in your worldly wisdom wrought they nil.

To feast upon that dying loathsome pain,
Where men had once disposed a deadly stain,
To lift the spoils of dusks, devout distill,
Where evening falls on those that you fulfill.

Sunrise Cloudburst

The Windswept Flower

This brazen act of madness known, to all of those who held their own,
As 'Tjeckers' was to be the source, of those who sold without remorse,
That ploughed the earth with wild discard, to reap rewards of low regard,
And tilled the ground for want of more, to which they boldly held the score.

But to the earth their fruitless quest, would lead them to a place of rest,
Where on the fences of our minds, the 'Tjeckers' bags would sadly find,
A place to hang; their gallant prize, was truth be known, not very wise,
But here tomorrow, from today, they hung for those to pick and pay.

The cost to those who would entrust, the sad lament of boom or bust,
Scant regard for those who weighed, nameless foods they oft displayed,
Life of those who would not steal, was empty with promise of a better deal,
They bravely stressed their offered right, to feast on spoils that they shop right.

Of those 'Tjeckers' bags that soiled, the land from which our brave men toiled,
The crop of men whom life had chosen, with chicken held in bags of frozen,
Plastic which so far afield, to hungry families they would hope to wield,
Ample work would not be marred; as to their homes, they would spar.

But what if those whose nature afforded,
could make a bag that history recorded.
That would by request an effort show,
a plant from which that bag would grow,
And seep in time to 'mother earth';
just what would our generation be worth?
The passing of that frenzied hour
that plagued us with that windswept flower.

Lonely is the man

Lonely is the Man, to whom the world appears to be,
Umpire to a life within secluded serendipity,
Cordon to a world which to a singular degree,
Is fated by a man-made law, to which they would decree

Fateful is the Man, to which the world would stand and claim,
Is limited to strife and grief to which they lay the blame,
Upon their own indulgences, which to him feels the same,
Would be their own misgiving want, for which they see the shame.

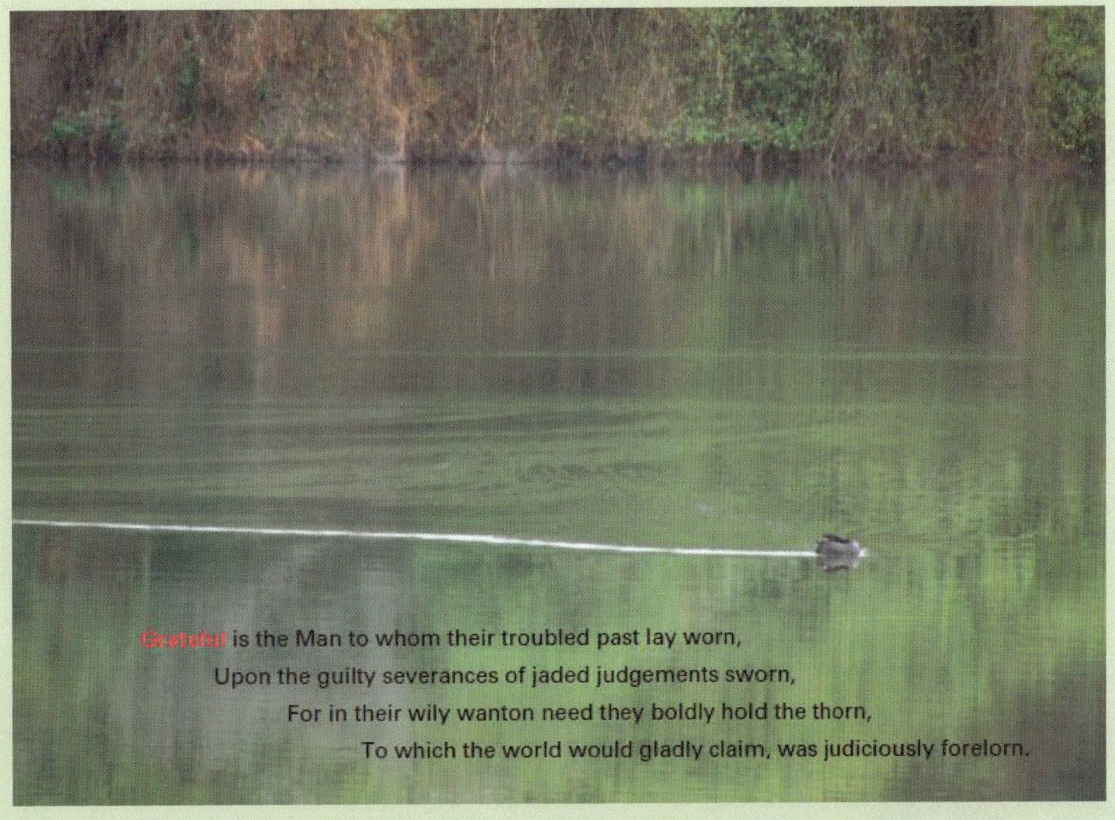
Grateful is the Man to whom their troubled past lay worn,
Upon the guilty severances of jaded judgements sworn,
For in their wily wanton need they boldly hold the thorn,
To which the world would gladly claim, was judiciously forelorn.

But happy is the Man, to whom this world will fade away,
And in the blessing of the Lord, his humble works to stay,
Would rise above those tailored rules to stretch beyond the fray,
Upon which idle hands will judge their own exclusive way.

For glorious is the fading moon which hides behind the cloud,
Foreshadows earth in ghostly pale, illumination is allowed,
So within darkened crevices its waning message loud,
The toils of Man the Lord beseeched would earnestly stand proud.

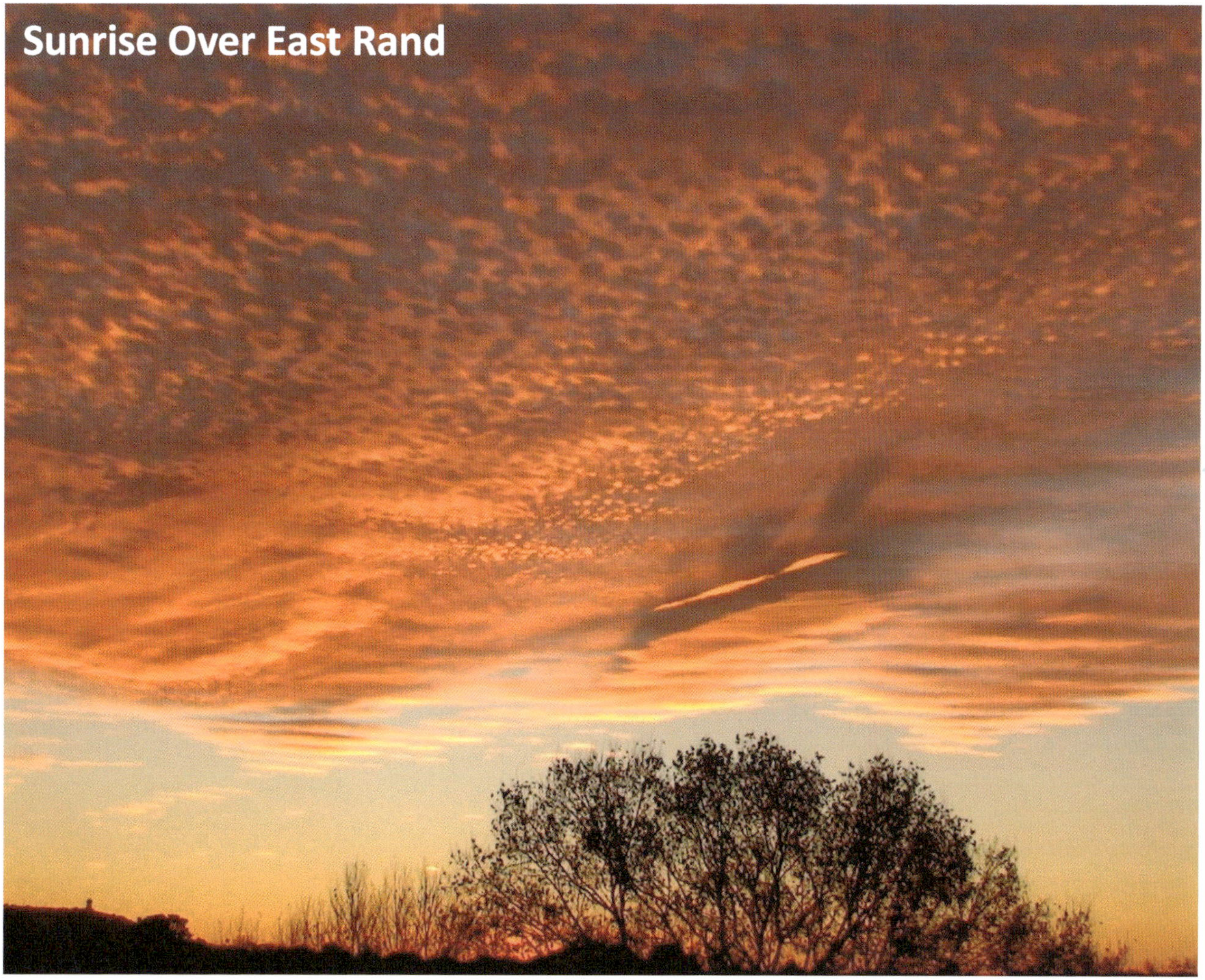
Sunrise Over East Rand

A Soliloquy

To know you all, is all that once had mattered,

The glass of fate, in dastardly deeds had shattered,

And all around me fall and feign with praise,

Deemed, in time the works my foil, they raise.

Yet herein lay the gross and deadly vice,

That once had harkened back to days, 'think twice',

Their actions speak of men that hold the key,

If only, to invoke soliloquy.

For therein lay the bold and keen advice,

Of men to whom this world would once entice,

With tales of grand and generous assurance,

Their haunting words to me would gain no durance.

For in those golden, lofty words of wisdom,

Remains the pearls of worlds beyond his Kingdom,

To gain the seat beside that vaunted throne,

Would once entail the faults that men are prone.

To scatter vulgar worldly seeds of sin,

Then gain the key to pearly gates within,

Would which, compel a sinful man to shed,

The failings of a life bereft and dead.

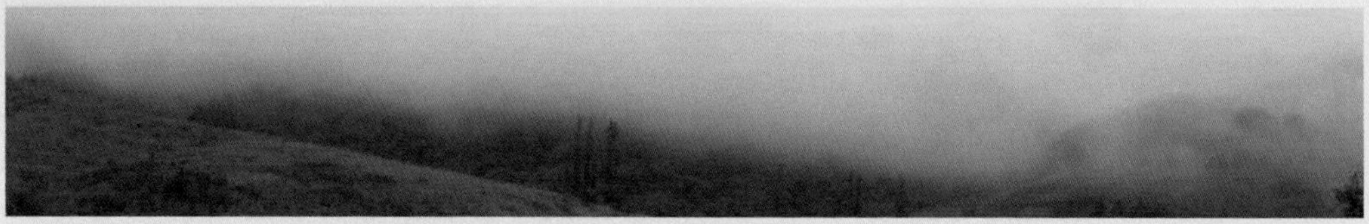

So thereon lay the crown devoid of stones,

That once would blind the weak and fragile tones,

That floated wild and sullied through the night,

At once, with that, which with my sin delights.

But gain ascendancy of power within,

For which the shadow cast away, is sin,

To live and work to praise that calm extreme,

His humble service I would not demean.

In all iniquity that once would pledge,
That he would take my sin aloft to dredge,
And gain the vast and spiritual oft sort realm,
To guide me from his tender loving helm.

THE GRAND ZAMBEZI

TO HIGH-SIDE ON THAT UNTAMED BEAST, TO STAND UPON THE PROW,
AND REACH TOWARDS THE THOSE VAULTED CLIFFS, AND TAKE A FINAL BOW,
AS TO THE DEPTHS BELOW THAT BOILING RAPID, IN HARMONY YOU PLOW,
TO MELT AMONG THE STEAMING TORRENT, YOU LIFT A FURROWED BROW.

AND PLUNGE WITHIN THAT HEAVING MASS, AND THROW WITH ALL YOUR MIGHT,
EVERY SINEW IN YOUR FRAME, THAT WITH ALL YOUR WEIGHT AND HEIGHT,
WILL CAST YOU IN THAT DEAFENING DIN, WITH SURGING FOAM YOU FIGHT,
AND RISE ABOVE THE RAGING FERMENT, TO GAIN WITHIN YOUR SIGHT.

AND CAST UPON THAT SEETHING SCUFFLE, MORE THAN JUST YOUR EYE,
FOR WITH YOUR SOUL YOU'LL RAISE THE GOAL, UNTO WHICH MEN DIE,
AS WAY WITHIN THAT SPIRITED FRAY, A LIGHT WILL SHINE TO DENY,
A LIFE MISSPENT OR POORLY LENT TO THINGS WHICH MEN BELIE.

FOR IN THAT CONFLAGRATION WILD, YOU SEE THE FINAL LIGHT,
AND EVER UPWARDS WILL RETURN, YOUR ENDLESS WILL TO FIGHT,
FOR IT IS SAID THAT OF THE BRAVE, THEIR CHALLENGE LAY IN SIGHT,
BUT FEW MEN VENTURE DOWN THAT PATH, AND TO THE END ALIGHT.

IN KEEPING WITH THE COURAGE BORNE,
THAT MEN WILL FIND AN INSIGHT,
IS THE CHALLENGE, TO THOSE OF US,
WHO WITH THEIR SIN WOULD IN SPITE?
DENY THE MAN, WHO THROUGH HIS LAND,
HAD FOUGHT TO CLAIM A RIGHT,
TO SHARE THE COMMON GLORY,
OF THAT GRAND AND VAUNTED BIRTH RITE.

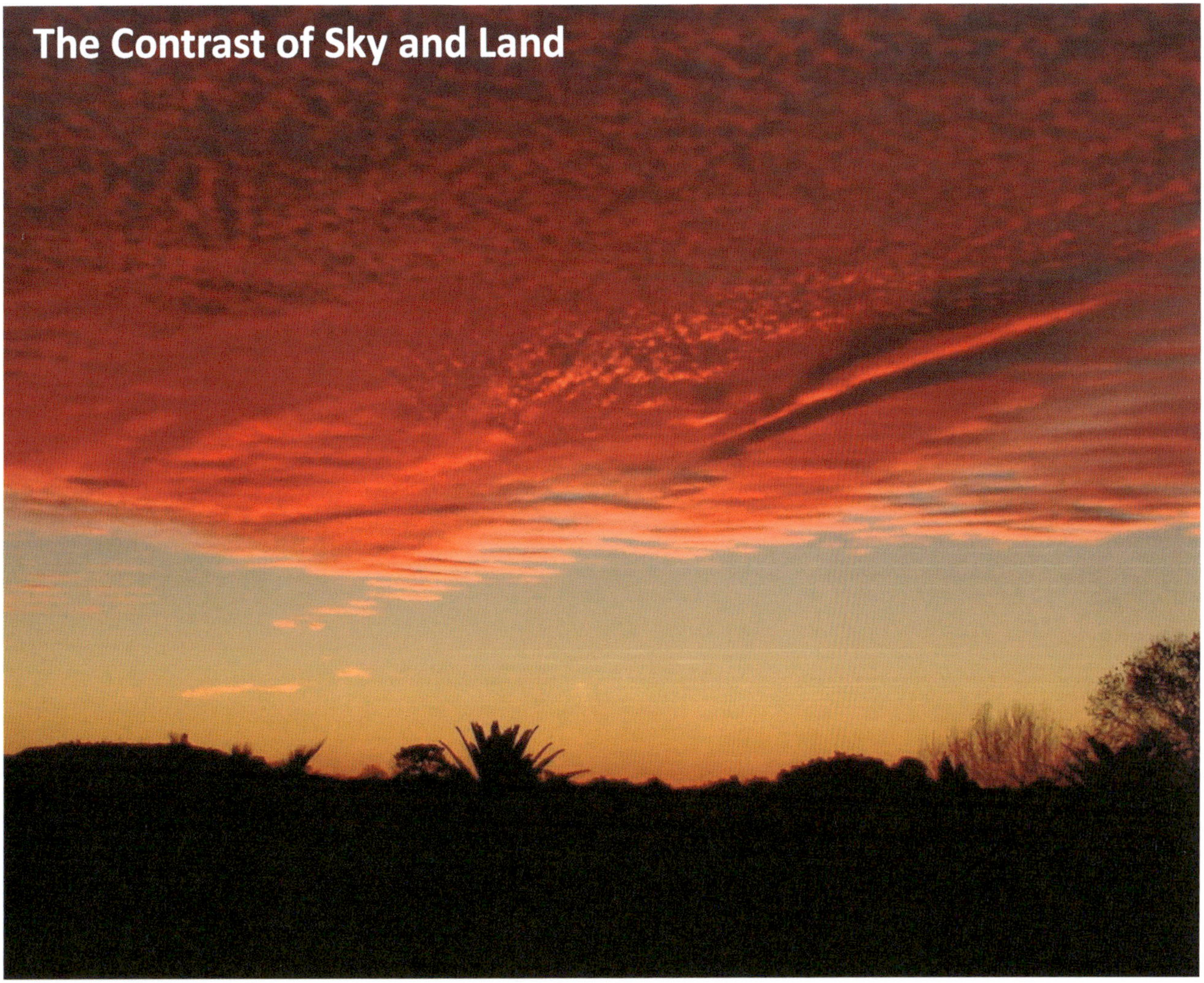
The Contrast of Sky and Land

And Lobengula Slept

Standing on that craggy granite rock, upon that vast foreboding plain,
The man looked down from his hilltop vantage, to survey with disdain,
Upon that sleeping, slothful Impi, with whom the Spirits raged,
Took his chances with one fell swoop, his mission was engaged.

And with the haunting burnished moon, beyond cloak and dagger cloud,
He slipped with ease amid the crevice, to which access allowed,
To steal and seek within murky cave, the wise man which he sought,
The Spirits beckoned with haughty cries, the damage they had wrought.

Through the embers of a smoldering fire, the cavern walls danced alive,
For way beyond the courage of some, their arrogance will survive,
So keeping with his knowledge borne, to the soulless Sangoma he crept,
And to his throat a blade he plunged, while Impi and Lobengula slept.

With blood-strangled cries of Spirits evoked, the shrill echo brought to life,
A flood of tears upon that land, their ancestors impaled with a knife,
The distant Impi roused beyond that cave, but ghosts had sealed their fate,
To jump to defend their lost cause would end, with the ashen body prostrate.

And in that distant time of yore, their destiny would hang on the thread,
Of a vanquished tribe, to which man inscribes, a litany of untold dead,
But the gauge of a nation, steeped in that blood, would rise again to be heard,
By the spilling of more, through the telling of truths, 'Gukurahundi' in a word.

The Great Zimbabwe Ruins

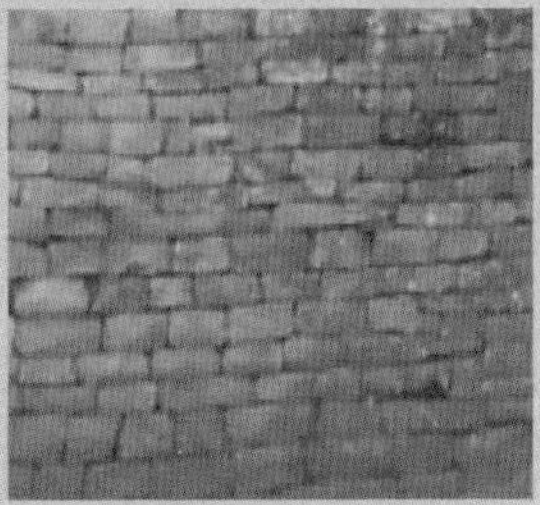

From every seeping banal wound, in each a gross and septic scar,
They came like puss through gaping holes to heal below a southern star,
The flock at once to break those bonds, that once interred their liberty,
That sore, a flood, their lives in truth, now a 'double jeopardy'.

For of that once and pristine land, bounteous silos they would hew,
The scourge of man had raised his hand, upon those bold and faultless few,
To them of whom the land **ingrained**, within their blood a tragedy,
The sickness spread a low refrained call to stem that parody.

The man to who they once revered, with shouts of clenched fist comradeship,
Would sell them on to pastures wild, to claim that land for ownership,
Amongst his loyal and grateful court, to play the royal jester,
He would to all his subjects claim, the role of grand investor.

But truth is somewhere past those claims, and time would be its master,
For when the rolling surge would clear, behind that hidden plaster,
The lesion that was once their mark, would like a scratch be shown,
And then the people might embark, to lands that men would hone.

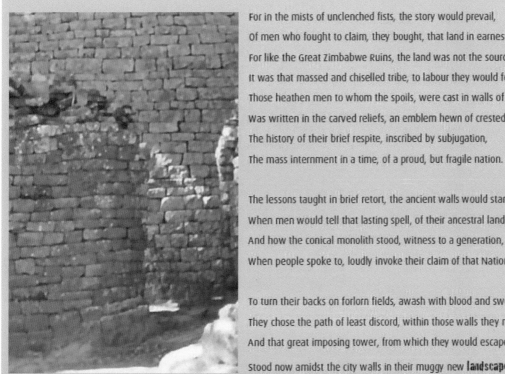

For in the mists of unclenched fists, the story would prevail,
Of men who fought to claim, they bought, that land in earnest sale,
For like the Great Zimbabwe Ruins, the land was not the source,
It was that massed and chiselled tribe, to labour they would force.
Those heathen men to whom the spoils, were cast in walls of granite,
Was written in the carved reliefs, an emblem hewn of crested flight,
The history of their brief respite, inscribed by subjugation,
The mass internment in a time, of a proud, but fragile nation.

The lessons taught in brief retort, the ancient walls would stand,
When men would tell that lasting spell, of their ancestral land,
And how the conical monolith stood, witness to a generation,
When people spoke to, loudly invoke their claim of that Nation.

To turn their backs on forlorn fields, awash with blood and sweat,
They chose the path of least discord, within those walls they met,
And that great imposing tower, from which they would escape,
Stood now amidst the city walls in their muggy new **landscape**.

And in a turn of bold events, of Biblical proportion,
Those ancient tribes to Man inscribes, a testamentary distortion,
Of servitude in lands imbued, with riches laden high,
And to their children would relay tales they would decry.

For every **Nation** on this earth, has stood the test of time,
Some would wane with low refrain, and some would rule sublime,
But in the pen of landless men, the truth would soon be told,
A story etched and boldly sketched, of slavery, they were sold.

Murambatsvina was to Him

They came from all surrounds with every tribe its Joseph story,
Of men to whom the world resounds with calls of sporadic glory,
For in those fables of a land that suffered tragic deprivation,
Was the legend of a man that held a brief but brutal station.

In some gross and vile respite, the Pharaoh of that land would fight,
And keep within his strength and might, all the land he held in sight,
To pledge the lives of all his folks and keep his kingdom for himself,
To send them with some evil hoax, to lands devoid of living wealth.

The pestilence of lives profound, with each new visitation,
Was like the punishment renowned, for loathsome habitation,
That like the King of Egypt then, would claim a revolution,
Murambatsvina was to Him, just such a great solution.

To push the people from the land, from which they had a claim,
The King would force the very source, for which he lay the blame
To flee their homes of worldly tombs, Generals had justification,
With all their power, they found the hour, to speed that evacuati

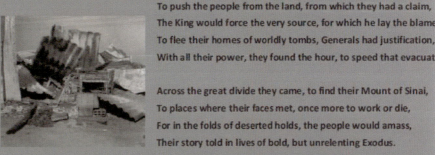

Across the great divide they came, to find their Mount of Sinai,
To places where their faces met, once more to work or die,
For in the folds of deserted holds, the people would amass,
Their story told in lives of bold, but unrelenting Exodus.

Silver on Silver

Encircled by their canvas encampment, a feisty display of defiance,
The volk had placed the children within, to claim a sense of reliance,
The women and men, in droves that came, foraged to make ends meet,
And in dusks delight, through camp firelight, they hastened a rapid retreat.

To homespun homes in their midst, of a necessity's dire invention,
Had heralded anew, those volk within, to re-claim their lost intention,
A community of sorts, would numbers import, a sense of sharing devotion,
And in the twilight, of a cool winter's night, they harkened to family devotion.

The evening meal in iron pots forged, traditions of culture cultivated,
The children were fed, and hastened within, men folks hunger satiated,
The women domestic, now huddled together, spoke in murmurs of respite,
Men folk engaged, through lost sense of rage, would speak of a future requite.

For in that dark maelstrom beyond the promise of a land once invoked,
Had shielded these volk, through trials within, a history idyllically choked,
The children astute, would listen intently, pre-slumber evoking those dreams,
Of a land that would shelter, under a helter-skelter canopy of star lighted beams.

Then in the flickering of history's bright fire, ancient ethnicity rekindled,
The relating of customs, in epic encounters, enabled the life that dwindled,
To recall the legends, relayed through these volk, replaced by modern devices,
Showing the past, could clearly surpass, the medium with which our life suffices.

An Ode to my Brother

To what does one owe, the treasure of a time,
When every waking minute, is riddled with that line,
What is the meaning to this life, and who does one call,
When in the moment of decision, you would walk so tall.

For each and every moment, was left for you to guide,
Where all those about you, from that mantle shied,
But in your strength of character, you held a steadfast stride,
So why was it you, my brother, and not me that died?
Who will do the striding on that lonely shore?
Why did that the sun set, on you forever more?
Unanswered was my prayer that called you to my side!
Time was the healer, your answer would provide!

So taking from my healing, the call to hold you fast,
With longing whisper to my God, that his grip would last,
For in that iron grasp I felt, it was from you that cast,
Every demon to the side, and rendered me aghast.

Taking from my spirit, and holding me so strong,
Was that message you implored, dragging me along,
But in the moment that I relent, to that powerful grip,
Was the realization that, we both could steer that ship.

1642

From the cautious protruding tongue of an Aardvark,
To the zymurgy of an Elephant's marula filled stomach,
Africa was alive with the possibility of its' favoured sons.
In a dichotomy of Darwinian delinquency that held, ones breath,
To the simplicity of a ritual throw of ancient bones on scorched mother earth,
The continent was cherished by its' inheritors.

In the frail but unvanquished child laying bloated in her mothers arms,
To the suited pin striped egotist laying comfortably in Suburban Utility Vehicles,
The landscape was awash with great hope and courage.

From the bold red bludgeoned hint of evenings' call.
To the foetus pink rise of a dawning sun that screams in contrast to his birth,
The African sky foretells its' liturgy.

From a fated sun rise on eastern shores, where gentle turtles hide their clutch,
To an emblazoned setting sun obscured below Koeburg silhouettes,
A precursor to the power our country would enlist.

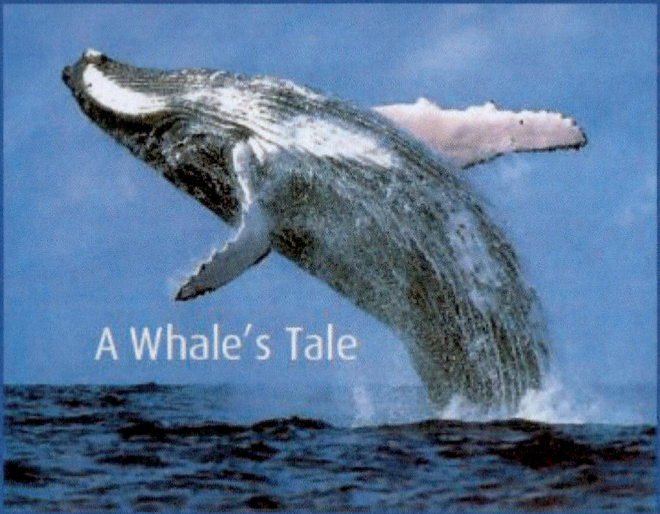
A Whale's Tale

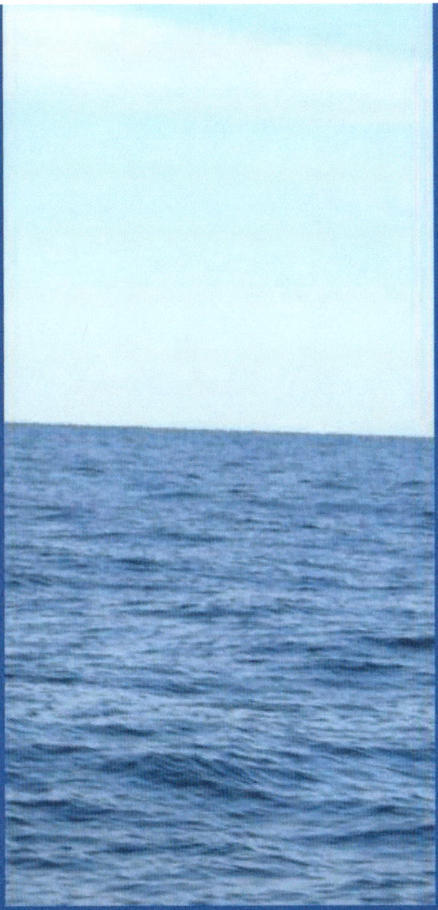

To breach the sapphire-blue and emerald-green,
Where once a weary visitor, weighed anchor,
A journey to the edge of worlds unseen,
The falsehood of this world would rancour.

Where aqua-blue collide the two must meet,
And all the earth shall shout for them to cease,
The ruin of that which lay beneath their feet,
And man may learn to live in virtual peace.

From saline ocean depths to azure sky, erupt,
The call to man a sign that they may trust,
Soul food to a nation hood at once corrupt,
They shout for all of those bereft and bust.

Then to the fragile ocean-green their ploy,
At one with nature, there they will entreat,
To those who would their world for all, destroy,
Lament and turn away from their defeat.

And of those ocean-depths from whence men crept,
The tale was borne of worlds at once sublime,
An epoch told of how our world had slept,
A mystery solved, but just in nick of time.

THE ELEPHANT AND ME

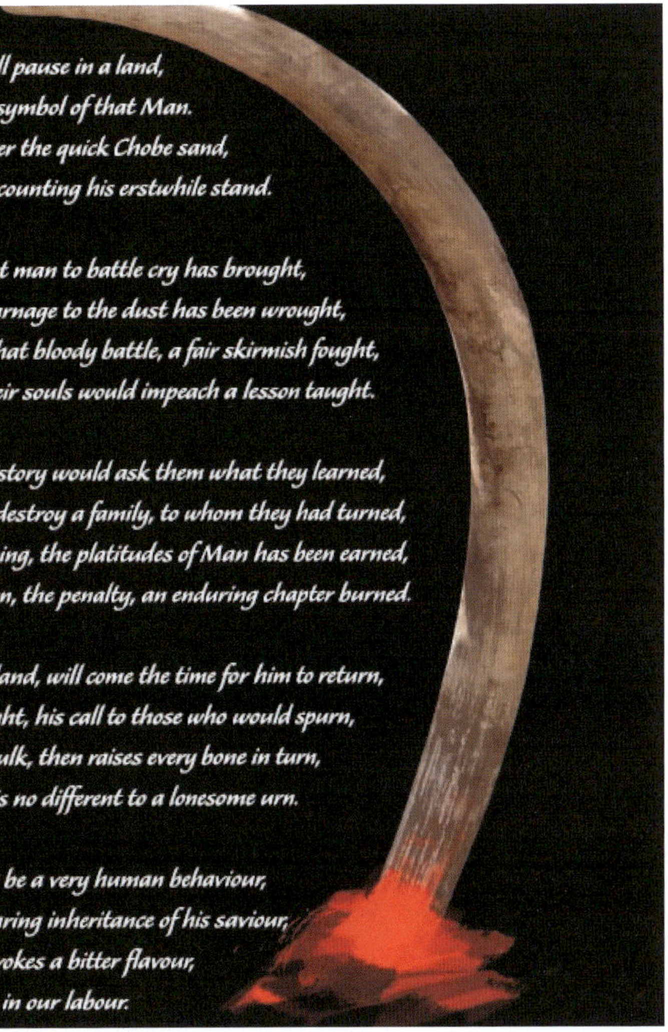

Weather worn and time forelorn, the Elephant shall pause in a land,
To be as a sage, time-honoured gauge, to reflect a symbol of that Man.
His war weary bones, white as the stones, that litter the quick Chobe sand,
But where-under he lies, battle-hardened skies, recounting his erstwhile stand.

Life he would defend, with his might to the end, but man to battle cry has brought,
Weapons that have sent, in sad disillusionment, carnage to the dust has been wrought,
For in the settling fray, in no uncertain way, was that bloody battle, a fair skirmish fought,
Alas, it must be said, of those abandoned dead, their souls would impeach a lesson taught.

For a life, so gentle, unrequited and sentimental, history would ask them what they learned,
That rendering to their own, all they had prone to destroy a family, to whom they had turned,
To face that moral warning with those of you fawning, the platitudes of Man has been earned,
The Elephant will stand, as a testament to the Man, the penalty, an enduring chapter burned.

But settled by the sand, that marks that distant land, will come the time for him to return,
And trumpet to those in sight, the havoc of his plight, his call to those who would spurn,
The shadow of his bulk, cast upon that deserted hulk, then raises every bone in turn,
For in that introspection, to man a soul reflection, is no different to a lonesome urn.

To hold aloft those he cherished oft, would seem to be a very human behaviour,
But in that mould, that man would hold, an endearing inheritance of his saviour,
Would seem to be an inconsistency, that to taste evokes a bitter flavour,
The Elephant and me, could hardly be, so different in our labour.

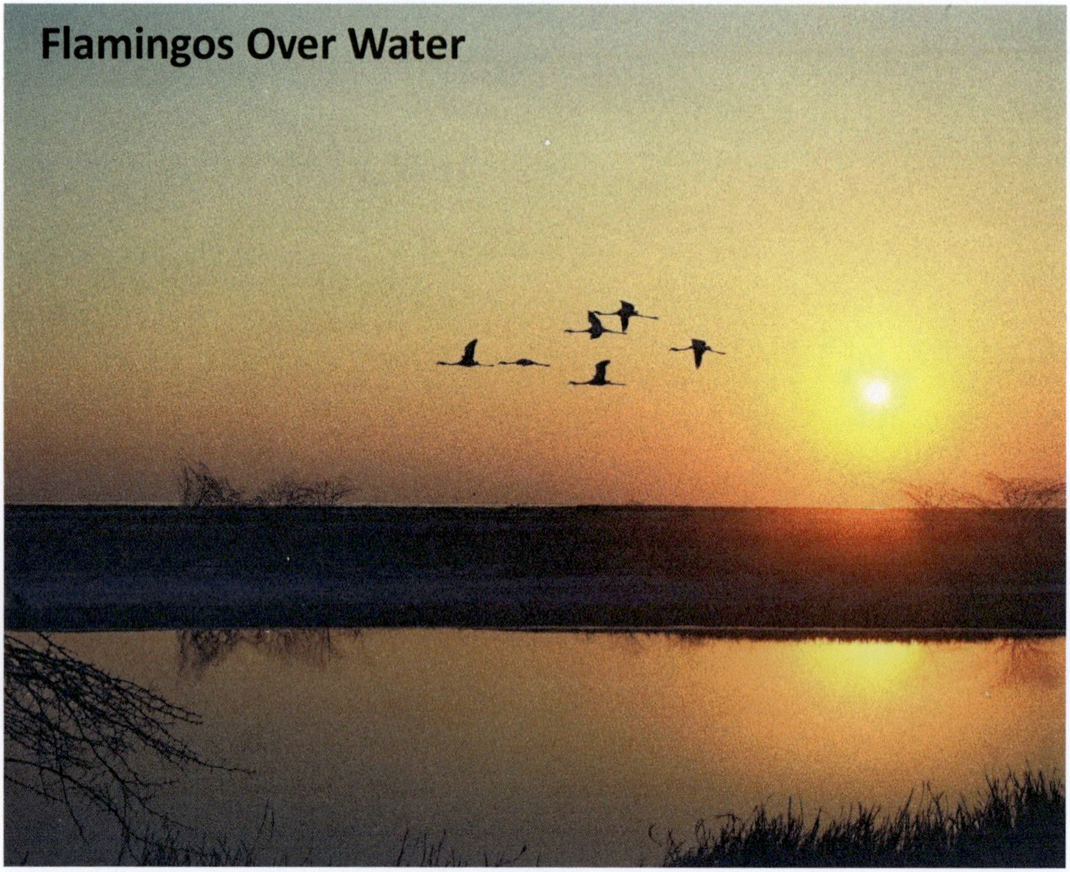
Flamingos Over Water

Borrowed Time

For every fleeting second of the next intake of breath,
For every passing minute that you view your life in depth,
On every hour, the hand will turn to watch your fragile health,
Will pass the day, that to yourself you breathe that living wealth.

For each and every week, with which your soul will gain that life divine,
The month to which you're life retreats is like the sands of time,
So be assured the year you hear, that last and lonely chime,
The clock will strike its final blow, to end the final line.

But don't believe that with that tone, you'll return to mother earth,
For in the living and breathing spirit, lives that fateful birth,
So each and every one of you might wish to treat with mirth,
The calling of a gentle voice, 'Come, see the kingdom of my worth'.

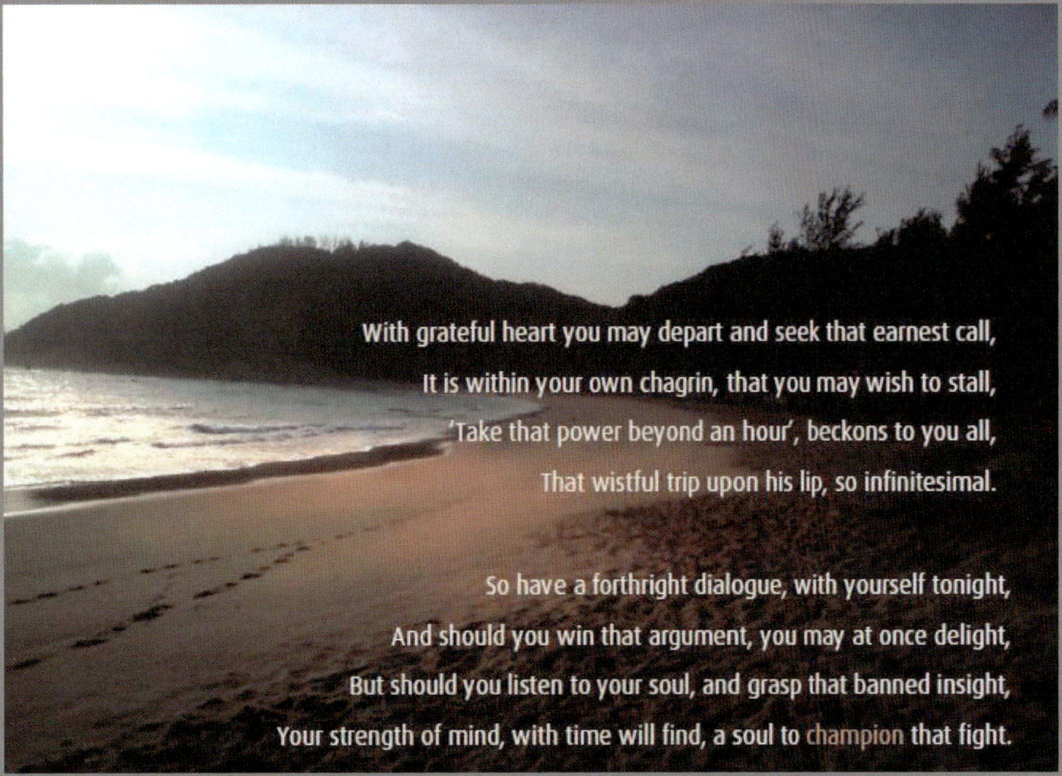
With grateful heart you may depart and seek that earnest call,
It is within your own chagrin, that you may wish to stall,
'Take that power beyond an hour', beckons to you all,
That wistful trip upon his lip, so infinitesimal.

So have a forthright dialogue, with yourself tonight,
And should you win that argument, you may at once delight,
But should you listen to your soul, and grasp that banned insight,
Your strength of mind, with time will find, a soul to champion that fight.

Moonlight, Monsters & Morality is an epic adventure through Africa, containing the landscapes that created the poems. Poems in which the story of Africa and its brutal history can be pictured in such grand poetic literature for the world to understand, and the people of Africa to remember why it is we live here! The vast panoramas of Zimbabwe, Malawi, and the sweeping coastlines of South Africa and the foreboding weather, are just a sample of the photography memorialised in these thought-provoking poems of a continent unmatched by any other. The poetic expression of an untamed wilderness and the men and women who have carved their homes out of its granite rock and forged such magnificent histories to be shared.

Printed in Great Britain
by Amazon

41888621R00053